FROM SEA TO SHINING SEA

ARKANSAS

ELLEN MACAULAY

Consultants

MELISSA N. MATUSEVICH, PH.D.

Curriculum and Instruction Specialist
Blacksburg, Virginia

RACHEL KAYE ACKERMAN

Director of Children's Services
Rogers Public Library
Rogers, Arkansas

CATHERINE J. HOWSER

Arkansas State Library
Little Rock, Arkansas

CHILDREN'S PRESS ®

A DIVISION OF SCHOLASTIC INC.

New York • Toronto • London • Auckland • Sydney • Mexico City
New Delhi • Hong Kong • Danbury, Connecticut

Arkansas is located in the south central part of the United States. It is bordered by Oklahoma, Texas, Louisiana, Mississippi, Tennessee, and Missouri.

The front cover photo shows the view from Mount Magazine.

Project Editor: Meredith DeSousa
Art Director: Marie O'Neill
Photo Researcher: Marybeth Kavanagh
Design: Robin West, Ox and Company, Inc.
Page 6 map and recipe art: Susan Hunt Yule
All other maps: XNR Productions, Inc.

Library of Congress Cataloging-in-Publication Data

Macaulay, Ellen.
        Arkansas / by Ellen Macaulay.
            p. cm. — (From sea to shining sea)
        Summary: Presents the geography, history, government, and people of Arkansas.
Includes bibliographical references (p.   ) and index.
 ISBN 0-516-22296-1
        1. Arkansas--Juvenile literature. [1. Arkansas.] I. Title. II. Series.
F411.3.M332002
976.7—dc21   2001008324

TABLE of CONTENTS

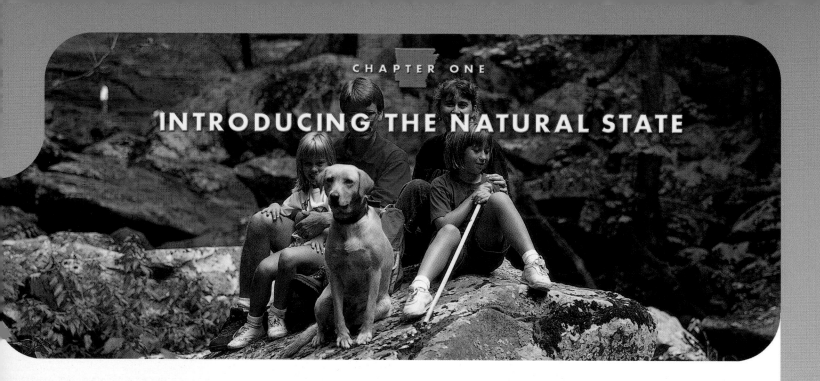

CHAPTER ONE

INTRODUCING THE NATURAL STATE

Hikers enjoy a beautiful summer day in the Ouachita Mountains.

Arkansas (ARK-an-SAW) is called "the Natural State" for good reason. Just picture green mountains, rolling plains, raging rivers, and crystal lakes. Add in soaring bald eagles, cascading waterfalls, and sparkling diamonds, and you'll begin to have an idea of all Arkansas has to offer.

Arkansas' attractions are often overlooked. Because it is bordered by six states (Texas, Oklahoma, Missouri, Tennessee, Mississippi, and Louisiana), Arkansas is a bit like the middle child in a large family—sometimes, it doesn't get enough attention! About the only thing many people know about Arkansas is that it is former president Bill Clinton's birthplace. You'll soon discover that there is so much more to this beautiful state.

Arkansas is a "middle" state in more ways than one. It ranks 27th in size and 33rd in population. Throughout its history, too, Arkansas has been at the center of things, including some our country's most important issues. Some people claim that the Civil War started in Arkansas. So did another kind of war—the Civil Rights Movement. Arkansas truly represents the heart of America.

What comes to mind when you think of Arkansas?

- Bird watching and fishing on Lake Chicot
- Dancing a jig at a folk arts and crafts fair in the Ozark Mountains
- Digging for diamonds in the Ouachitas
- Cheering for the University of Arkansas Razorbacks
- Getting steamy at Hot Springs National Park
- Canoeing on the Buffalo National River
- Exploring limestone caves throughout the Ozarks
- Wondering at the ancient Toltec Mounds

Have you ever heard the expression, "a diamond in the rough"? It describes something that hides a rare beauty within. That's how it is with Arkansas. Chip away at the outside to discover what's inside—a treasure of a state!

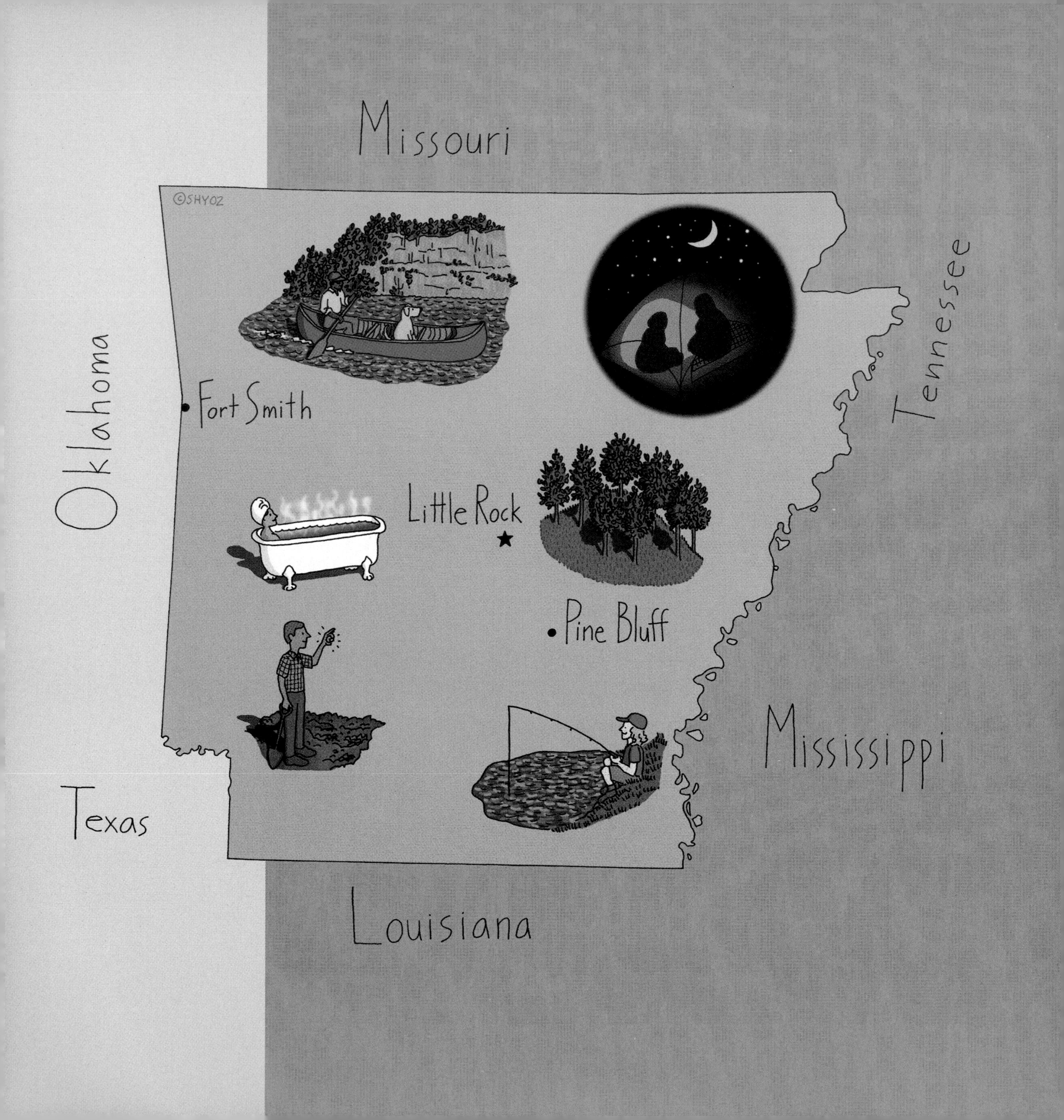

Missouri

Oklahoma

Tennessee

©SHY02

• Fort Smith

Little Rock
★

Pine Bluff

Texas

Mississippi

Louisiana

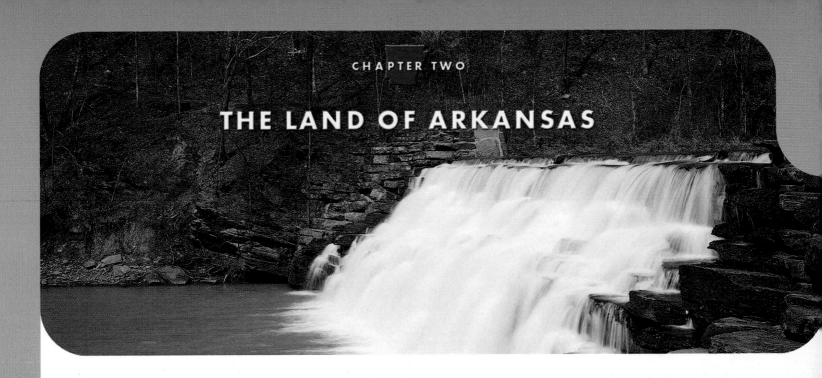

CHAPTER TWO

THE LAND OF ARKANSAS

The song "America, the Beautiful" could have been written just for Arkansas. Its mild climate makes it a pleasant place to live, and its fantastic geography makes it a fun place to visit. Do you like fishing, swimming, white-water rafting, mountain climbing, and birdwatching? All these activities and more await you in Arkansas.

Arkansas is a state of both forests and water. More than half the land is wooded. There are also more than 600,000 acres (242,811 hectares) of lakes and almost 10,000 miles (16,093 kilometers) of streams, rivers, and natural springs. Three of its major rivers form natural borders: the Mississippi River divides Arkansas from Tennessee and Mississippi, and the Red River separates part of Arkansas from Texas. Also, the St. Francis River forms a small part of Arkansas' border with Missouri.

The scenic beauty of Devil's Den State Park is typical of many parts of Arkansas.

Arkansas' geography changes dramatically from place to place. The land naturally divides into four regions: the Ozark Plateau, the Ouachita Province, the West Gulf Coastal Plain, and the Mississippi Alluvial Plain.

Ozark Plateau

The highland area of the Ozark Plateau covers the northwestern portion of Arkansas. The limestone Ozark Mountains run through parts of Oklahoma, Missouri, and Illinois, as well as Arkansas. Originally formed by the erosion (wearing down) of three giant plateaus tens of thousands of years ago, the ancient Ozarks are distinguished by rough terrain and many tucked-away caves.

FIND OUT MORE

How does water carve through a solid mountain to create bluffs? How long might this process take?

Although many people visit the Ozark Mountains, they remain unspoiled and pollution-free.

The powerful, white water of the 132-mile (212-km) Buffalo National River carved out the towering bluffs (steep cliffs) of the Boston Mountains, which form the southern border of the Ozark Plateau. Only the most experienced rafters dare take on the wild water through these rocky gorges. Another major river in this region is the White River, located in the northern Ozarks. Surrounding lakes include Bull Shoals Lake, Beaver Lake, and Norfork Lake.

The Ozark region is world-famous for its cold springs. Cold springs are natural pools of mineral water that bubble up through cracks in the earth. Spring water is healthful to drink. Pure Ozark water is bottled and sold in stores throughout the world. Mammoth Spring is Arkansas' largest natural spring. Nine million gallons of water flow through the spring every hour.

More than 2,000 limestone caves are found throughout the Ozarks. These caves are ancient—more than 10 million years old! You may explore the sparkling formations of many of these wondrous caves. The Ozarks are so vast and rugged, there are still caves yet to be discovered.

FIND OUT MORE

Stalagmites, spelunkers, and stalactites are all found inside caves. Look up these words in a dictionary. Which of these words could be describing *you*?

The rock formations inside Blanchard Springs Cavern were formed over millions of years, and they are still slowly changing.

Ouachita Province

This mid-Arkansas region lies south of the Ozark Plateau, on the western side of the state. The Ouachita Province is home to the Arkansas River Valley and the sandstone Ouachita Mountains. There you'll find meadows, streams, cascading waterfalls, and rolling green hills. Also in this region are the five Diamond Lakes, including Lake Ouachita, and the Ouachita River, a river wide enough for large ships to travel on. Can you guess the name of the 225-mile- (362-km-) long hiking trail through the Ouachita Mountains? It's the Ouachita Trail!

Fishermen enjoy a peaceful day on Lake Ouachita, nestled in the hills of the Ouachita National Forest.

The Arkansas River Valley was carved out centuries ago by the Arkansas River, the largest river in Arkansas. The Arkansas River flows east across the state, through the capital city of Little Rock, and into the Mississippi River. From Artist Point, a spot overlooking the Arkansas River Valley, the view is spectacular. In fact, Artist Point has been called the "Grand Canyon of the Ozarks," in reference to Arizona's famous Grand Canyon.

The Arkansas River Valley is also home to the stunning River Valley Tri-Peaks. It is named *Tri*-Peaks because there are three distinct mountains: Mount Nebo, Petit Jean Mountain, and Mount Magazine, which,

You can get a good view of the Arkansas River Valley from Pinnacle Mountain, which rises more than 1,000 feet (305 m) above the valley.

Visitors can hike and sight-see at Mount Magazine State Park.

at 2,753 feet (839 meters), is Arkansas' highest peak. Ecologists call Mount Magazine "The Galapagos of Arkansas" because, like the Galapagos Islands in South America, many unique animals are found there. About 127 species of colorful butterflies alone have been identified on Mount Magazine.

To the south of the Arkansas River Valley lie the Ouachita Mountains. These mountains were created more than 300 million years ago, when the earth's crust was still forming. As a result, the mountains have a unique folded appearance, looking something like a paper fan. The Ouachitas are the only mountains in the United States with ridges that run east to west; all others stretch from north to south.

Hot Springs National Park is home of the Ouachita's famous thermal springs. There, the water temperature of the springs reaches a toasty 143° Fahrenheit (62° Celsius). Early Native Americans believed the hot springs had healing powers. They used the spring water to bathe their sick and wounded. Today, people consider the hot springs a kind of health center. They still bathe in the hot springs. Others simply like to breathe in the steam to clear their lungs.

The beautiful Ouachitas are the only place in North America where you can find diamonds. Crater of Diamonds State Park contains a natural volcanic pipe filled with minerals, quartz crystals, and diamonds, where people can come and search for jewels. More than 70,000 diamonds have been discovered there so far.

West Gulf Coastal Plain

The West Gulf Coastal Plain covers the southwestern portion of Arkansas, where the sandy Mississippi Alluvial Plain and the Arkansas River meet. The West Gulf Coastal Plain is also known as the Timberlands,

A young girl searches for diamonds at Crater of Diamonds State Park.

13

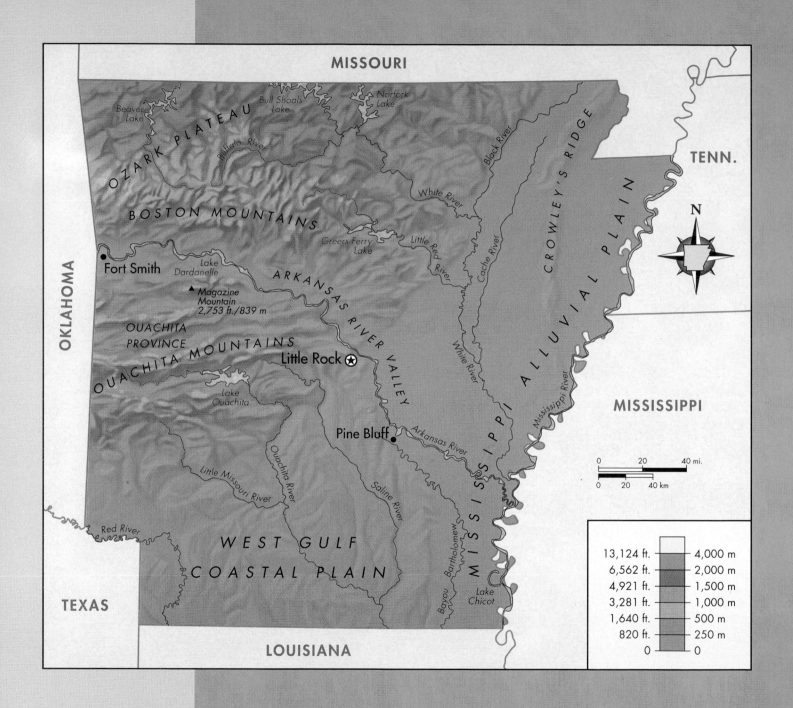

MISSOURI

Beaver Lake

Bull Shoals Lake

Norfork Lake

OZARK PLATEAU

Buffalo River

BOSTON MOUNTAINS

White River

Black River

CROWLEY'S RIDGE

TENN.

N

Fort Smith

Lake Dardanelle

Greers Ferry Lake

Little Red River

Cache River

ARKANSAS RIVER VALLEY

▲ Magazine Mountain 2,753 ft./839 m

OUACHITA PROVINCE

OUACHITA MOUNTAINS

Little Rock ✪

White River

MISSISSIPPI ALLUVIAL PLAIN

Mississippi River

MISSISSIPPI

OKLAHOMA

Lake Ouachita

Pine Bluff ●

Arkansas River

Little Missouri River

Ouachita River

Saline River

Red River

Bayou Bartholomew

Lake Chicot

WEST GULF COASTAL PLAIN

0   20   40 mi.
0   20   40 km

TEXAS

LOUISIANA

13,124 ft.	4,000 m
6,562 ft.	2,000 m
4,921 ft.	1,500 m
3,281 ft.	1,000 m
1,640 ft.	500 m
820 ft.	250 m
0	0

because of its plentiful supply of timber. The West Gulf Coastal Plain is filled with lush pine forests containing many natural resources—not only timber, but oil and natural gas as well.

The Saline (meaning *salty*) River flows from the Ouachita foothills to the Ouachita River. The protected area surrounding the river is known as the Felsenthal Refuge. The refuge provides a safe home for the endangered red-cockaded woodpecker. In the winter, another important visitor arrives—the American bald eagle. The bald eagle is also endangered.

The West Gulf Coastal Plain is a lush area spotted with lakes, rivers, natural springs, and wetlands such as bayous (marshy streams). Bayou Bartholemew is the longest bayou in the world. It is 341 miles (549 km) long, 300 miles (483 km) of which flow through Arkansas.

A bald eagle takes flight.

Mississippi Alluvial Plain

The Mississippi Alluvial Plain makes up the eastern portion of Arkansas. Its eastern border is the Mississippi River, a major waterway for many states including Arkansas' next-door neighbors, Tennessee and Mississippi. The region's western border roughly follows the Spring River to where it meets the White River. The White River flows through the farmland area of the Mississippi Alluvial Plain.

The Mississippi Alluvial Plain is what many people think of when they picture the Deep South—miles and miles of swampy flatlands as well as some mighty big bugs, too! The constant flooding of the Arkansas

Bald cypress trees grow in the swampy Moore Bayou.

and Mississippi Rivers contributed to the swampy environment, with one benefit. This flooding created rich, deep alluvial soil. Alluvial soil, packed with minerals from the river, is perfect for growing crops. Most of Arkansas' farming is done right here in the Mississippi Alluvial Plain.

In the midst of the far-reaching flatlands of the Mississippi Alluvial Plain is Crowley's Ridge. Crowley's Ridge consists of 200 miles (322 km) of skinny hills rising 100 to 250 feet (30 to 76 m) in the air. The

Crowley's Ridge is a popular recreational area.

ridge was formed by pressure from glaciers, water, and wind over the past 50 million years. Described as a "genuine world oddity," Crowley's Ridge is also a beautiful recreational area. It is covered with wildflowers and oxbow lakes. Oxbow lakes are U-shaped. They are formed when a river changes course.

Southwest of Crowley's Ridge is the White River Refuge. This refuge contains 350 lakes, including Arkansas' largest natural body of water, Lake Chicot, an oxbow lake. Bird watchers from around the world flock to this area.

CLIMATE

Arkansas has a comfortable climate. It is warm in the summer. Temperatures range from 80° to 90°F (27° to 32°C), the hottest areas being in the southeast. It is mild in the winter. Winter temperatures seldom drop below 30°F (−1°C). There is little snowfall, only about 6 inches (15 cm) a year, mostly in the northern Ozarks. However, Arkansas gets plenty of rain—44 to 48 inches (112 to 122 cm) of rain falls each year through most of the state, and about 10 inches (25.4 cm) more in the southeast.

The hot, humid weather from March to June occasionally produces destructive tornados—whirling funnels of air that can reach speeds of up to 500 miles per hour (805 kph). If the funnel touches the ground, the movement of the air can do serious damage to homes, people, and anything else in its way. Arkansas had a series of tornado activity in the winters of 1996 and 1997, in which 26 people were killed.

CHAPTER THREE

ARKANSAS THROUGH HISTORY

The first people living in present-day Arkansas were Native Americans called Bluff Dwellers. Bluff Dwellers lived in the hidden Ozark caves about 12,000 years ago, sharing their habitat with wolves, saber-toothed tigers, and bears. Archaeologists (scientists who study objects from the past) have uncovered evidence of their lives, including human bones, stone tools, primitive weapons (spears), and petroglyphs, or cave drawings. One group of Bluff Dwellers, called Archaic hunters and gatherers, primarily stayed in the Ozark bluffs. The Paleo group eventually spread out all over Arkansas.

From A.D. 600 to 1050, a group of people called the Mound Builders thrived in Arkansas. This Native American society centered around towering earth mounds made of dirt, gravel, and sand. A few of these amazing structures still exist at Toltec Mounds Archeological State Park near

This scene shows the budding town of Hot Springs in the late 1800s.

19

You can explore ancient Native American mounds at Toltec Mounds Archeological State Park.

Little Rock. Although the tallest one remaining is 49 feet (15 m) high, archaeologists believe that the original mounds were much taller.

Native American groups such as the Caddo, Quapaw, and Osage also lived in the area we now call Arkansas during this early period. The Quapaw lived in the southeast on the lower Arkansas River, and the Caddo lived along the Southwest Red River. The Osage, a warring group, hunted in the Ozarks. Other Native American groups, including the Cherokee and the Choctaw, arrived centuries later in the late 1790s.

The Nodena people were another advanced civilization (A.D. 1350 to 1700). These Native Americans were farmers. Artifacts, or objects from the past, show that theirs was a complex society of art, religion,

FIND OUT MORE

Archaeologists are not certain what purpose the earth mounds served. They have uncovered bones, tools, and pottery on platforms (for climbing) and in rooms built into the Toltec Mounds. Why do you think the Mound Builders created these mounds?

government, gardening, and trading. A Nodena site has been preserved at Hampson Museum State Park near Wilson, Arkansas.

EUROPEAN EXPLORERS

In 1541, Hernando de Soto and his Spanish explorers crossed the Mississippi River to become the first Europeans in what is now Arkansas. De Soto was looking for gold. Instead, he found the Ouachita hot springs.

During his two years in Arkansas, de Soto visited a Parkin village (present-day Parkin Archeological State Park). He was surprised at what he found. This Native American society, dating back to A.D. 1000, was not what the Europeans had imagined at all. Instead of teepees, the Parkin people had built sturdy, permanent huts. They hunted and grew their own food, including crops such as corn, beans, and squash. They built ceremonial mounds. In addition, they were concerned with security. The 17-acre (7-ha) village was surrounded by a moat and a heavy log wall that offered protection from warring groups.

The Parkin people were not afraid of the Spanish. They welcomed them into their village.

This drawing by Oscar Berninghaus shows DeSoto and his expedition seeing the Mississippi River for the first time.

What they didn't realize was that outsiders carried diseases such as measles and smallpox. The Native Americans had no resistance to these European germs. So many natives died from these diseases that by 1550 the Parkin village was deserted.

It wasn't until 1673 that the next group of visitors arrived in Arkansas. Seven explorers floated down the Mississippi to the mouth of the Arkansas River. They were led by two Frenchmen, Jesuit missionary Father Jacques Marquette, and a fur trader, Louis Joliet. The explorers were met by friendly Quapaws. The Quapaws warned them about the fierce Osage, frightening Marquette and Joliet enough to make them leave Arkansas in search of safer territories.

La Salle claimed the Mississippi River Valley for France in 1682.

In 1682, French explorer René Robert Cavelier, Sieur de La Salle and his group came to a nearby Quapaw village. The Quapaw again treated the French strangers with kindness. They fed them and gave them shelter. However, La Salle did not seem to appreciate their charity. He even called them "savages" in his writings. La Salle went on to claim the entire Mississippi River Valley for France, including the land of Arkansas. He named the area *Louisiana* in honor of King Louis of France. La Salle left Arkansas soon after his arrival to explore further west.

An Italian fur trader named Henri de Tonty came in search of La Salle. In 1686, de Tonty established the first permanent European settlement on the banks of the lower Arkansas River, called the Arkansas Post. Arkansas Post served as a central fur-trading center and a protected area for French travelers. At the time, beaver fur was extremely valuable in Europe, where it was used to make fashionable clothes and hats. Arkansas, as well as the surrounding areas, had a plentiful supply of beavers. Fur traders traveled to the post, conducted their business, and moved on to new areas. De Tonty was the first to introduce his fellow Europeans to the land of Arkansas. For that reason, he is often called "The Father of Arkansas."

The gentle Quapaws and the Europeans shared and traded furs and food. Some even married. It was, for some time, a peaceful and successful co-existence.

Native Americans traded furs in exchange for clothing, tools, and weapons.

By the 1700s, the word had spread. Arkansas (still called Louisiana) had a lot to offer—plenty of food and water; wide, open spaces to build shelter; and furs to trade. People from Europe and the East Coast arrived and settled in different areas. German farmers chose the Mississippi alluvial plain area for its rich soil. Scots (people from Scotland, a European country) preferred the Ozarks, perhaps because it reminded them of the highland homes they left behind.

By 1717, the fur traders had moved on to new conquests, leaving the settlers behind. Without the traders, the post fell on hard times. The Quapaw tried to help by giving the settlers food. Still, many people died. The settlers simply didn't have the experience needed to survive tough conditions such as bad weather, lack of shelter, and dangerous wild animals.

LOUISIANA PURCHASE

Between 1763 and 1800, France and Spain had both owned the land of Arkansas at one point or another. Neither country, however, was very involved with this small part of the large Louisiana territory. It was a simple competition between the two countries.

In 1803, when France claimed ownership, United States President Thomas Jefferson sent statesman James Monroe to Paris. Jefferson wanted him to persuade the French to sell eastern and western Florida and New Orleans to the United States. Tired of competing with Spain over the faraway territory, France agreed. The French surprised Jefferson by offering to sell not only Florida and Louisiana, but all the land west of the Mississippi River to the Rocky Mountains. President Jefferson quickly agreed. The deal was called the Louisiana Purchase. The Louisiana Purchase cost the United States $15 million. If you think that's a lot of money now, imagine how much it was back then! It was well worth the money, however—the Louisiana Purchase doubled the size of what was then the United States.

After the sale, Arkansas was no longer referred to as Louisiana. Instead, it was considered part of the Missouri Territory. The Arkansas Post became its first capital. By 1819, there were 14,000 settlers, enough to create a separate territory called the Arkansas Territory.

After the Louisiana Purchase, laws were quickly passed to meet the needs of the developing territory. In 1821, the capital was moved from

President Jefferson signs an agreement for the Louisiana Purchase. Thirteen states would later be carved out of the Louisiana Territory.

WHO'S WHO IN ARKANSAS?

William E. Woodruff (1795–1885) was born on Long Island, New York. In 1819, he arrived at Arkansas Post and immediately started Arkansas' first newspaper, the *Arkansas Gazette*. Woodruff both wrote and printed this influential (important) paper. The *Arkansas Gazette* became the oldest newspaper west of the Mississippi.

the soggy, malaria-ridden Arkansas Post to Little Rock, a rough-and-tumble frontier town with barely 20 people. Little Rock was chosen for its central location to the Arkansas River. Little Rock has remained Arkansas' center of government ever since.

In 1824, Arkansas established its first road, called the Southwest Trail. The trail ran through Little Rock to the Red River and was used by pioneers traveling to Texas. Some famous folks walked this road, including James Bowie, creator of the Bowie knife; Sam Houston, future president of the Republic of Texas; and Davy Crockett, a colorful frontiersman identified by his coonskin hat.

TRAIL OF TEARS

Whether by oxcart, keelboats, or steamships, westward-bound settlers streamed through the Arkansas Territory. For those who chose to stay in Arkansas, land ownership became an important issue. Settlers refused to share with the Native Americans who had lived there freely for so many years. The settlers wanted the land for themselves. The United States government sided with the white settlers, and pressured Native Americans to give up their land.

As early as 1818, gun-toting Europeans forced out the Quapaw and Osage. Later, it was the Cherokee. Men, women, and children had to leave their whole way of life behind. In 1838, the United States Army forced Native Americans to move west to Indian Territory (present-day Oklahoma) to live on government reservations (areas set aside for Native

American groups). This sad route, which the Cherokee and other Native Americans took across Arkansas to Indian Territory, was named the Trail of Tears. By 1840, tens of thousands of Native Americans had walked the Trail of Tears. More than 4,000 of them died on the march.

With only a few moments notice, many Native Americans were forced to leave their homelands east of the Mississippi River to move west.

FROM TERRITORY TO STATE

On June 15, 1836, the Arkansas Territory became the state of Arkansas—the nation's twenty-fifth state. Arkansas got its first state governor, James S. Conway; state senators, Ambrose H. Sevier and William S. Fulton; and a congressional representative, Archibald Yell. Little Rock remained the capital.

WHAT'S IN A NAME?

The names of many places in Arkansas have interesting origins.

Name	Comes From or Means
Arkansas	Originally closer to *Akansea*, it is an Algonquian word (a Native American language) for the Quapaws meaning "south wind"
Little Rock	Named for an actual little rock in the Arkansas River that was used as a landmark
Mount Magazine	Named *Magazin* by French hunters, meaning "store-house"
Ouachita	Name of a Native American group originally from Louisiana; meaning of the name remains unknown
Ozark	From French "aux arcs," whose meaning is unclear. Possibilities: "from among the Arkansas" or "with bows"
Petit Jean	French for "Little John"
Quapaw	Downstream people (living near where the river flows)

During this time, Arkansas' African-American population was also growing, although not by choice. Like other southern states, Arkansas practiced slavery. Slaves were Africans who were snatched from their native country and brought to the New World (the American colonies) on ships. Once there, they were forced into slavery on farms and plantations, which often meant a hard life of labor and abuse.

By the 1800s, slavery was common in some parts of Arkansas. According to the new state's laws, however, all slaves in Arkansas were to be freed. There was just one catch—slaves were freed only with the consent of the slave owners. Most slave owners simply ignored the new law. In 1836, Arkansas' population had grown to more than 50,000. By 1840, the population would double. African-Americans numbered 20,000.

CIVIL WAR

Times were prosperous during the 1850s. Steamboats and stagecoaches brought goods and more people into Arkansas. As new towns and businesses went up, forests were cut down just as quickly, increasing the risk of flooding. Not surprisingly, lumber mills thrived as did lead, iron, and coal mines. Cotton, grown along the Mississippi River and picked by slaves, became a major crop.

The cotton industry in Arkansas was highly dependent on slaves.

Things ran smoothly until Abraham Lincoln was elected president in 1860. He wanted to abolish (do away with) slavery. The southern states, however, refused to do so. Their way of life was highly dependent on farming and slave labor, and they couldn't imagine making a decent living otherwise. Many Southerners felt that by taking away their right to own slaves, the government was favoring the North.

To protect their rights, the South was willing to go to war. Of the more than 430,000 Arkansans (about 100,000 of whom were slaves), most were simple farmers who didn't even own slaves, yet some of these people agreed it was each state's right to make its own laws. They didn't want the United States government telling them what to do.

In protest, several southern states seceded, or withdrew, from the United States. At first, the people of Arkansas voted against secession. After more debate (spirited discussion), however, enough people

FIND OUT MORE

How did Arkansas' varied geography provide hiding places for supplies and weapons? How about for surprise attacks and quick retreats? (One answer: think Ozark caves.)

The Battle of Pea Ridge was one of the first major Union victories of the Civil War.

changed their votes that the decision was reversed. In May 1861, Arkansas seceded from the United States and joined the other southern states to form a new nation called the Confederate States of America, or the Confederacy.

About 60,000 men and boys left their farms and families to fight for the South. Other Arkansans—about 15,000—refused to support the Confederacy and joined the Northern (Union) forces instead. It was Arkansans against Arkansans, Americans against Americans. The bloody Civil War (1861–1865) was the darkest period in the short history of the United States.

Arkansas was the site of several key battles during the Civil War. In March 1862, an important battle was fought in Pea Ridge, when the Confederates tried to occupy Missouri. The battle was so closely fought, it wasn't entirely clear at first which side won, but history gives the victory to the Union army. The Battle of Pea Ridge was the largest battle fought west of the Mississippi.

On July 4, 1863, the Battle of Helena was fought to gain control of the Mississippi River. A keen blow to the Confederates came in September of 1863, when the Union captured Little Rock. Confederates set up a new capital at Washington in Hempstead County, while Arkansans who sided with the North established their own government in Little Rock.

In April 1864, the Confederates scored a needed victory. In what came to be known as the Red River Campaign, they won three key battles in south central Arkansas. Winning the battles of the Red River Campaign shut down the Union's complete conquest of Arkansas. For a change, the Union armies were forced to retreat across the flooded Saline River.

In 1865, the Confederates surrendered, and the war was over. Arkansas set about rejoining the United States. They changed their state laws to go along with the United States Congress, after which Arkansas was readmitted to the United States in 1868.

In a short time, Arkansas went through five constitutions (the official laws and rulings of the state) in 1836, 1861, 1864, 1868, and 1874. The Civil War (and the slavery issue) created most of the changes. Although the slaves were freed as a result of the war, African-Americans were still not entirely free. Hated and feared by many whites,

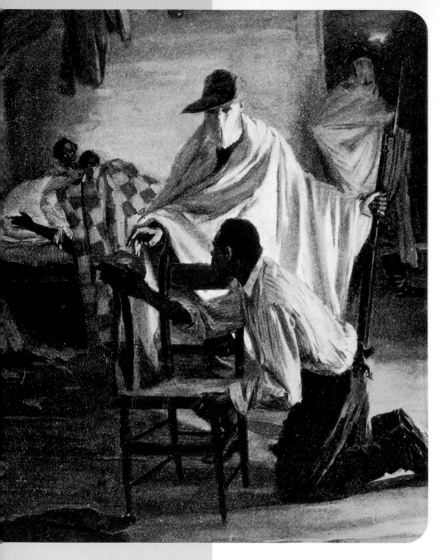

Hate groups, such as the Ku Klux Klan, sprang up all over the South. Their members attacked and murdered African-Americans during the late 1800s.

African-Americans were victims of hostility and violence. Many of the changes in Arkansas' constitutions were attempts to secure basic human rights for African-Americans such as the right to an education, the right to vote, and the right to free use of public places.

RECONSTRUCTION

The Civil War cost Arkansas lives and resources. Many soldiers returned home to find their farms in ruin. The United States tried to rebuild the South and help reorganize the governments of the southern states by providing aid and money. This period was called Reconstruction.

Some Northerners took advantage of the trouble brewing in the South—including Arkansas—after the war. These people were called carpetbaggers because they carried their possessions in large carpet-covered bags. Carpetbaggers roamed the countryside searching for bargains. They bought property that was lost by Southerners and then tried to sell it back at a huge profit. Many Southerners couldn't afford to buy their own homes back. By the 1880s, when the United States government was no longer handing out money to buy southern property, the carpetbaggers were gone. Many chose to stay in the South rather than return North.

Some Southerners, as well, took advantage of other people's misfortunes. Landowners rented out their land to freed slaves and poor whites, called tenant farmers. Tenant farmers paid rent in the form of crops, which left them with few crops for themselves. Often, tenant farmers ended up with hardly enough money to live on. This became a new form of slavery called sharecropping. Arkansas remained bitterly poor for years to come.

As Arkansas entered the 1880s, trouble arose. Farm prices were at an all-time low during the 1880s and 1890s, and the farmers blamed the railroads. By 1890, 2,200 miles (3,541 km) of railroad tracks crossed the state (except for the isolated Ozarks). The railroads not only brought in more settlers, they also made it easier to sell products and to haul lumber as far west as San Francisco. As a result, people didn't have to rely on local farms anymore, and farm prices went down.

Despite the farmers' problems, it was clear that the government favored the railroad industry. Many government officials were connected with the railroad, which was a profitable industry. To pro-

Carpetbaggers were portrayed as greedy businessmen who took advantage of Southerners.

EXTRA! EXTRA!

In April 1874, Arkansas experienced a colorful piece of history. When Elisha Baxter was elected governor of Arkansas in 1873, his opponent, Reverend Joseph Brooks, claimed that Baxter cheated on the vote counting. In protest, Brooks marched into the governor's office, grabbed the newly elected Governor Baxter, and threw him outside! Brooks then made himself at home in the governor's chair. Baxter wasn't about to go away quietly, however—he set up his own governor's office outside. The "Brooks-Baxter War" went on for a month until President Ulysses S. Grant stepped in to settle the dispute. He declared Brooks out, and Baxter back in.

tect their own interests, farmers got together and formed a political party called the Agricultural Wheel, or the Wheelers. In 1900, the farmers pulled off a victory when Jeff Davis was elected governor. Although Davis had not been a Wheeler, he agreed with their ideas and plans. Davis controlled big business and gave farmers an equal chance. He also introduced new labor laws and stopped wasteful spending.

Jim Crow laws were another big problem for the South, including Arkansas. Jim Crow laws were designed to keep African-Americans "in their place," meaning separate from whites. For example, even though the United States Constitution gave African-Americans the right to vote, Jim Crow laws limited this and other rights. The laws also prevented African-Americans from using the same public facilities as whites. For example, they attended separate schools and were not allowed in many restaurants. Many Jim Crow laws were passed after the Civil War in response to the freeing of the slaves. Many more would be passed over the next hundred years.

By 1900, when the cotton picker came into common use, many African-American workers were forced to leave the farms in search of

A man drinks from a water fountain labeled, "For Colored Only." "Colored" was a term used to refer to African-Americans.

work. This turned out to be a blessing in disguise. In the cities, African-Americans found more supporters and their own political power.

THE RICH LAND OF ARKANSAS

In the late 1800s, the lumber and mining industries were booming. In 1887, an important discovery was made when bauxite ore was found near Little Rock. Bauxite is used to make aluminum.

By 1900, cotton was the leading industry in Arkansas. Rice, soybeans, fruit, livestock, and poultry were common products as well. A

Nebraska farmer, William H. Fuller, raised the first successful rice crop in Arkansas (near Carlisle) in 1904. Rice went on to become Arkansas' most important crop for some time, until it was replaced by soybeans.

The early 1900s brought more exciting discoveries. In 1906, John Huddleston found diamonds on his Murfreesboro farm. He sold his land, diamonds and all, for a large profit. A diamond mine was set up at the site. It was the only such mine in North America. A discovery of another kind was made in 1921. There were cries of "Black Gold!" when oil was found near El Dorado. It seemed that Arkansas was rich with oil fields. Some lucky folks became very wealthy as a result.

At the turn of the 20th century, people began to gather in bustling towns such as Texarkana and Fort Smith to look for work or fun. Life got pretty wild and dangerous in these parts. Gambling, drinking, and gunfights were common activities. Soon the lawbreakers outnumbered the law-abiding

EXTRA! EXTRA!

The largest diamond ever found was 40.35 carats—practically a boulder! It was discovered by the Arkansas Diamond Company in 1924 at Murfreesboro, in what is now the Crater of Diamonds State Park.

citizens. These towns became identified with the Wild West period.

HARD TIMES

The state's economy was better than ever in the early 1900s. Mechanical cotton pickers such as the cotton gin (invented in 1793) were now commonly used. Cotton gins automatically cleaned the seeds from the cotton, a job that was previously done by hand. Because the cotton gin made the process faster, tons more cotton could be exported by steamboat and railroad. Arkansas soon became the nation's leading producer of cotton and rice.

Prosperity didn't last long, however. In 1917, the United States entered into World War I (1914–1918). The United States government established a camp for soldiers near Little Rock. It was called Camp Pike in honor of Civil War general Albert Pike. About 70,000 Arkansans fought and helped European countries such as France and England to win the war against Germany, Austria-Hungary, and Turkey.

In 1927, floods devastated the state. The tremendous flooding started with the overflow of the Mississippi River. The flooding got so bad that

EXTRA! EXTRA!

Judge Isaac C. Parker (1838–1896) was assigned to serve in Fort Smith, Arkansas in 1875 (his courtroom is shown above). To children, he looked like Santa Claus, but to outlaws, life under his stern rule was anything but Christmas. His jail—always packed with wrongdoers—was known as "Hell on the Border." For over 21 years he dished up 9,500 convictions and sentenced 172 people to death, half of these by his favorite form of punishment—hanging. He is forever known as the "Hanging Judge."

(opposite)
The discovery of oil in El Dorado in 1921 transformed what was once a sleepy, small town into a boomtown.

A Red Cross volunteer
hands out food to drought
victims in Lonoke, Arkansas.

A Red Cross volunteer hands out food to drought victims in Lonoke, Arkansas.

water soon covered one-fifth of the state. Valuable crops, including cotton, were destroyed. Cotton prices dropped. The floods ruined farms. In the 1930s, too much water was followed by the opposite problem—too little water, or a drought. Many Arkansans gave up altogether and left for the promise of a better life in California.

Then, a period of hard financial times called the Great Depression (1929–1939) overwhelmed the United States, including Arkansas. The Great Depression caused money values to drop dramatically. People all over the United States lost their jobs, and in Arkansas, farm prices fell even further.

WAR ABROAD

The Great Depression ended as World War II (1939–1945) began. The United States entered the war in December 1941 when, in a sneak attack, the Japanese bombed a United States naval base at Pearl Harbor, Hawaii. More than 200,000 Arkansans served overseas in World War II. Back home, Arkansas' aluminum and oil industries filled the wartime need for more metal and fuel. Suddenly, there were more jobs and more money for the Arkansas people.

After the Japanese bombing, many Americans feared Asian people. Many Japanese-American families across the country were forced to leave their homes and live at supervised camps until the war was over. In 1942, two Japanese-American Relocation Camps were established in Arkansas—Rohwer and Jerome. Each camp held about 8,500 people. Life in these camps was not pleasant. It was hot and buggy, and snakes roamed the area. To pass the time, some Japanese Americans built artistic monuments. Two of these are preserved at the Rohwer cemetery, where many of the internees who died are buried. Shortly before the end of World War II, the Japanese-American families were moved out of the camps to make room for German prisoners of war.

During World War II, many Japanese-Americans were held at prison camps like Rohwer Relocation Center, located in McGehee.

After the war, many unemployed farm workers moved to cities to work in factories. From the 1940s to the 1950s, the number of factories doubled. In 1953, Arkansas was officially nicknamed the "Land of Opportunity" to help encourage new manufacturing industries and business headquarters to locate there. The new nickname meant that Arkansas welcomed new people and would help them get a new

FIND OUT MORE

The forced movement of Japanese-Americans wasn't the first time a group of people were forced to "relocate." Do you think history repeats itself? Could this happen again in the United States?

start. By the 1960s, manufacturing outperformed agriculture. With 1,786,272 people, Arkansas' population was again on the rise.

WAR ON THE HOME FRONT— CIVIL RIGHTS

During the 1950s, African-Americans across the South were struggling to gain their rights as citizens, called civil rights. In many parts of the United States, they were often denied the simplest rights such as using public water fountains or taking a seat on the bus. Most were not provided a chance for an education. The few African-Americans who attended school were always kept separate from white children. This practice of separating blacks and whites was known as segregation.

Many people felt that this kind of treatment was unfair. In an effort to undo this wrong, people of all races started working toward better treatment of African-American citizens. This was called the Civil Rights Movement.

In 1957, Arkansas found itself in the heart of the Civil Rights Movement. Three years earlier, in 1954, the United States Supreme Court had ruled against segregation. In response to the court ruling, President Dwight D. Eisenhower ordered that all public schools (previously separated according to blacks and whites) should be open to everyone, or desegregated. Although desegregation had been so ordered, the ruling allowed the states to decide for themselves when and where they would desegregate.

LITTLE ROCK CENTRAL HIG

Army troops escorted nine African-American students into Little Rock Central High School for the very first time.

In 1957, six African-American girls and three African-American boys (known as the Little Rock Nine) enrolled in the all-white Little Rock Central High School. There was just one problem—Arkansas Governor Orval E. Faubus didn't want to let them in. He called in the state National Guard to prevent them from entering. It wasn't until President Eisenhower himself stepped in that the students were finally allowed to enter; he sent United States Army troops to personally escort the African-American students to school.

The trouble didn't end there. Many white students continued to hassle and threaten the new students. They yelled and threw things at them. They carried signs with sayings like "Save Our Christian America." But the students never gave up. This explosive incident transformed the ordinary city of Little Rock into a symbol of discrimination for the entire nation. It was a turning point for civil rights, and one of the most important events in Arkansas history. In 1999, all nine African-American students received the Congressional Gold Medal for "selfless heroism" from President Bill Clinton, an Arkansan himself.

During the 1960s, racial violence continued throughout the South. The horror of these acts and the unfairness of the Little Rock Nine incident inspired many people to work for civil rights. People from around the nation came to Arkansas and the rest of the South to participate in events supporting civil rights. Protests of segregated schools continued. By the end of the 1970s, most (but not all) schools were

Several white students walked out of Little Rock High to protest the admission of African-Americans.

desegregated. It had been a long, hard fight, but progress had been made in Arkansas.

BALANCING INDUSTRY AND THE ENVIRONMENT

A movement to protect the environment began in the 1950s and 1960s. Arkansans had discovered that the logging and poultry plants that were so profitable had also created problems—they had polluted much of Arkansas' waters. Efforts were made to convince these industries and others to stop dumping waste into the waters.

There was also controversy surrounding the Buffalo River. Many people wanted to dam the river to prevent flooding and create lakes. Others (the environmentalists) wanted the river to run free. The environmentalists won in 1972, when President Richard Nixon declared the Buffalo River the first federal river, meaning that it would be protected by the government as a natural river. Hot Springs was the first national park in Arkansas, Petit Jean was the first state park, and Crowley's Ridge was the first national scenic byway. In the 1990s, due to its progress in preserving its beautiful environment, Arkansas became known as "The Natural State."

The Buffalo River was declared the first national river in 1972.

During the 1970s and through the 1990s, more people moved to Arkansas. The 1970 Arkansas River Program allowed ships to travel across the state from the Mississippi River to the Arkansas River. This development brought more business and money into Arkansas.

In the 1990s, Arkansas started advertising to attract businesses. The campaign has worked. Numerous Fortune 500 headquarters (the top 500 companies in the United States) are now located in Arkansas. Many other businesses, small and large, are leaving the soaring costs, traffic, and pollution of other states to come to Arkansas. Cities are growing and more jobs are available. Today, Arkansas' future looks brighter than ever.

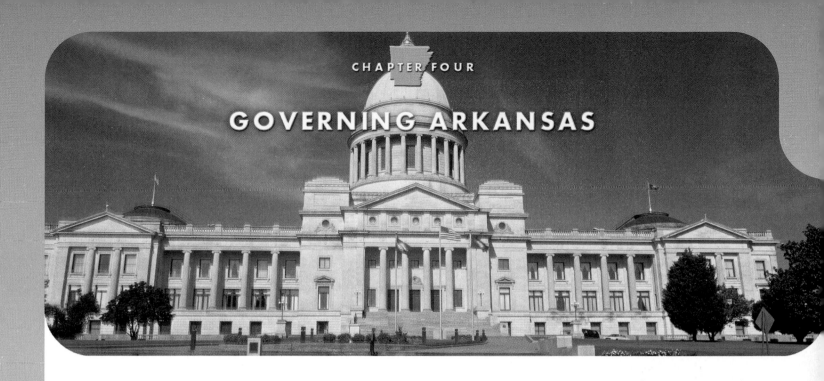

CHAPTER FOUR

GOVERNING ARKANSAS

Arkansas contains many counties. There are 75, to be exact, every one of which is divided into four main parts—Northeast, Northwest, Southeast, and Southwest. All of these counties have many people, all with different needs. For example, the farmers of the Mississippi Alluvial Plain might think a farming-related issue is important, while the lumberjacks of the West Gulf Coastal Plain, the artists of the Ozarks, and the businesspeople in Little Rock may disagree. It is a real challenge to govern any state, especially a state with as much variety as Arkansas. Everyone works together to do a good job.

The state constitution is especially important when it comes to governing Arkansas. This document outlines the system of laws under which the state will operate. After four earlier versions, Arkansas' present constitution was adopted in 1874. The constitution divides Arkansas' government into three branches—the executive, the legislative, and the judicial.

The Arkansas state capitol was built between 1899 and 1915.

The legislative branch makes the laws. The executive branch carries out the laws. Finally, the judicial branch interprets the laws.

EXECUTIVE BRANCH

The executive branch includes seven elected officials, including the head of state—the governor. Governors in Arkansas used to serve a short two-year term. Since 1986, that term has been increased to four years. Governors may be reelected once.

The other six constitutional officers are also elected for four-year terms, including the lieutenant governor, the secretary, the treasurer, the attorney general, the auditor, and the commissioner of state lands. Even though the governor is head of the executive branch, he or she also plays an important part in the legislative process (the passing of new laws). The governor has the power to veto (stop) the passing of a law that he or she does not approve of.

LEGISLATIVE BRANCH

The state legislature is called the General Assembly. It is Arkansas' lawmaking group. The General Assembly has two houses, or parts—a 35-member senate and a 100-member house of representatives. Senators serve a four-year term and may be reelected once. Representatives serve a two-year term and may be reelected twice.

The senators and representatives work part-time for the state; most hold other jobs outside of their legislative work. As legislators, they work to create new laws on issues such as crime, the environment, taxes, and commendations (such as honoring a local hero).

JUDICIAL BRANCH

The judicial branch interprets, or explains, the laws through the court system. The highest, or most important, court in the judicial branch is the state supreme court, which acts as head of the state judicial system. The supreme court consists of a chief justice (judge) and six other justices, all elected to eight-year terms. The supreme court hears appeals from lower courts. An appeal is an attempt to change a decision or ruling that was made in a lower court. The court of appeals hears these cases before they reach the supreme court.

Many cases begin in circuit court. The circuit court system hears both criminal and civil cases. Civil cases involve disputes over property, documents, and labor, among other things. Criminal cases involve crimes such as murder, drugs, or theft. There are 20 circuit court districts in Arkansas. Each circuit court judge serves a four-year term.

The Arkansas house of representatives meets inside the capitol building.

49

ARKANSAS STATE GOVERNMENT

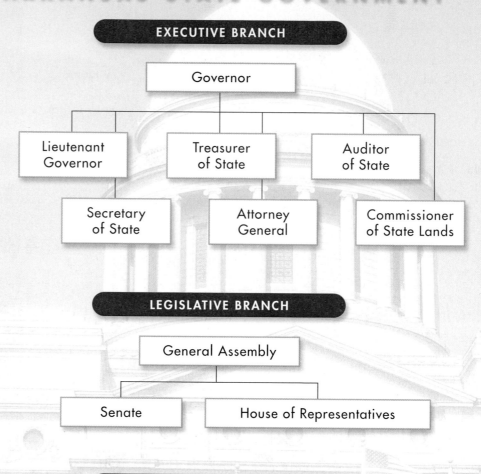

EXECUTIVE BRANCH

Governor

- Lieutenant Governor
- Treasurer of State
- Auditor of State
- Secretary of State
- Attorney General
- Commissioner of State Lands

LEGISLATIVE BRANCH

General Assembly

- Senate
- House of Representatives

JUDICIAL BRANCH

- Supreme Court
- Court of Appeals
- Circuit Courts
- Chancery and Probate Courts

ARKANSAS GOVERNORS

Name	Term	Name	Term
James S. Conway	1836–1840	George W. Donaghey	1909–1913
Archibald Yell	1840–1844	Joseph T. Robinson	1913
Samuel Adams (acting)	1844	J. M. Futrell (acting)	1913
Thomas S. Drew	1844–1849	George W. Hays	1913–1917
John S. Roane	1849–1852	Charles H. Brough	1917–1921
Elias N. Conway	1852–1860	Thomas C. McRae	1921–1925
Henry M. Rector	1860–1862	Tom J. Terral	1925–1927
Harris Flanagin	1862–1864	John E. Martineau	1927–1928
Isaac Murphy	1864–1868	Harvey Parnell	1928–1933
Powell Clayton	1868–1871	J. M. Futrell	1933–1937
Ozra A. Hadley (acting)	1871–1873	Carl E. Bailey	1937–1941
Elisha Baxter	1873–1874	Homer M. Adkins	1941–1945
Augustus H. Garland	1874–1877	Ben T. Laney	1945–1949
William R. Miller	1877–1881	Sidney S. McMath	1949–1953
Thomas J. Churchill	1881–1883	Francis Cherry	1953–1955
James H. Berry	1883–1885	Orval E. Faubus	1955–1967
Simon P. Hughes	1885–1889	Winthrop Rockefeller	1967–1971
James P. Eagle	1889–1893	Dale Bumpers	1971–1975
William M. Fishback	1893–1895	David Pryor	1975–1979
James P. Clarke	1895–1897	William (Bill) Clinton	1979–1981
Daniel W. Jones	1897–1901	Frank D. White	1981–1983
Jeff Davis	1901–1907	William (Bill) Clinton	1983–1992
John S. Little	1907	Jim Guy Tucker	1992–1996
John I. Moore (acting)	1907	Mike Huckabee	1996–
X. O. Pindall (acting)	1907–1909		

The chancery court system hears mostly property and family related cases. Each chancery court judge serves a six-year term. There are also other court-appointed officers, including county judges, municipal (public) judges, and justices of the peace. The 75 county judges also act as the county's business manager (they handle the county's money). These judges work with the justices of the peace to approve the county budget (how much money they can spend).

TAKE A TOUR OF LITTLE ROCK, THE STATE CAPITAL

The Old State House is a National Landmark, and the oldest surviving state capitol west of the Mississippi River.

The history of Arkansas' capital, Little Rock, dates back to 1722, when French explorer Bénard de la Harpe came in search of a mythical green emerald. What he found instead were two ordinary rock piles lying on opposite sides of the Arkansas River—one big and one small. Later explorers chose the small rock as a traveler's landmark. Since then, Little Rock has grown into a sophisticated city with more than 180,000 people.

The first state capitol, called the Old State House, was completed in 1842. It served as the capitol until 1911, when government offices were moved to the current capitol. In 1996, the Old State House was renovated and it is now a museum. This white, antebellum-style building makes for an impressive setting. It was there that Bill Clinton announced he was running for president, and where he made his two victory speeches.

The current state capitol looks very much like our nation's Capitol in Washington D.C., only smaller. In fact, this building has served as a stand-in for the more famous capitol in movies. Prisoners helped construct the building, which took 16 years to complete. The exterior is made of limestone that was quarried in Batesville, and the front doors are made of bronze. Inside, marble was used on the floor, walls, and columns of the rotunda, a round entrance room. The senate and house chambers are inside the capitol, as well as the old supreme court chamber, which has been restored to its original appearance.

Downtown Little Rock is a fascinating mixture of old and new. The Quapaw Quarter dates from the late 1800s and is the oldest part of the city. The dozen or so buildings making up the Historic Arkansas Museum Restoration show what life was like in Arkansas before the Civil War.

The Little Rock Zoo, containing hundreds of animals, is a popular site. Stroll along Riverfront Park for a great view of the Arkansas River. You'll find plenty of food treats at the River Market District.

This historic home is in the Quapaw Quarter. Every spring, many of the homes in Quapaw are open for tours to celebrate the area's heritage.

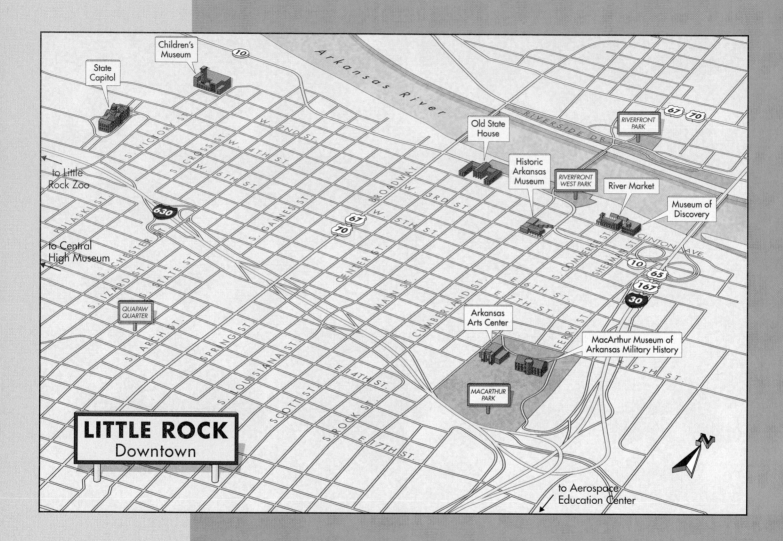

Children's Museum

State Capitol

10

Arkansas River

RIVERSIDE DR.

Old State House

67 70

RIVERFRONT PARK

W. 2ND ST.

S. VICTORY ST.

CROSS ST.

S. CROW ST.

W. 4TH ST.

W. 6TH ST.

Historic Arkansas Museum

RIVERFRONT WEST PARK

River Market

Museum of Discovery

to Little Rock Zoo

BROADWAY

W. 3RD ST.

PULASKI ST.

630

S. CHESTER ST.

S. GAINES ST.

67

70

W. 5TH ST.

CLINTON AVE.

COMMERCE ST.

SCOTT ST.

to Central High Museum

S. IZARD ST.

STATE ST.

CENTER ST.

MAIN ST.

10

65

167

30

QUAPAW QUARTER

S. ARCH ST.

SPRING ST.

S. LOUISIANA ST.

CUMBERLAND ST.

E. 6TH ST.

E. 7TH ST.

SHERMAN ST.

Arkansas Arts Center

MacArthur Museum of Arkansas Military History

FERRY ST.

E. 9TH ST.

E. 4TH ST.

SCOTT ST.

S. ROCK ST.

MACARTHUR PARK

E. 7TH ST.

LITTLE ROCK
Downtown

N

to Aerospace Education Center

Many people still visit David Owen Dodd's grave (the Boy Martyr of the Confederacy) at Mt. Holly Cemetery. At MacArthur Park, you can visit the Old Arsenal Building, birthplace of another hero, famous World War II general Douglas MacArthur. Today the Old Arsenal is home to the MacArthur Museum of Arkansas Military History. The Arkansas Arts Center, another one of Little Rock's many museums, is also in MacArthur Park.

Other museums include the Central High School Museum Visitors Center, where you can relive the history of the civil rights movement. The exhibits are interactive. For space fans, there's the Aerospace Education Center, complete with its own IMAX Theater. Little Rock also has places just for kids, including the Children's Museum of Arkansas and the Museum of Discovery.

As you stroll through Little Rock, don't forget to stop and smell the roses. It won't be hard to do—so many people grow roses there that Little Rock's nickname is the "City of Roses."

CHAPTER FIVE

THE PEOPLE AND PLACES OF ARKANSAS

Arkansans enjoy cheering for local baseball and other sports teams.

More than 2.6 million people live in Arkansas. Just over half of those people live in or near the big cities of Little Rock, Hot Springs, and Pine Bluff. Many others live in the northwest Arkansas cities of Fayetteville, Springdale, Rogers, Bentonville, and Fort Smith. Some folks prefer the quiet, country life of the rural areas across the state.

The vast majority of Arkansans—about 8 in every 10 people—are descendants of the original European settlers. The next largest ethnic group is African-Americans, who make up about 16 of every 100 people. Also, more and more Hispanic Americans are locating in Arkansas, making up roughly 3 of every 100 people. Rogers, a community in northwest Arkansas, has one of the fastest-growing Hispanic populations in the United States. Fewer than one in every 100 people (1%) are Asian or Native American. Most of the Native Americans are Cherokee who live in the northwest. There are no other organized Native American groups left in Arkansas.

Arkansans are known to be a religious people. A large portion of the population attends worship services and bible classes. Most Arkansans are Protestant, while others are Baptist or Catholic. There are many churches throughout the state, ranging from the fancy (a gilded cathedral in Little Rock) to the simple (an open-air gathering spot in an Ozark forest).

Arkansas has a down-home reputation. Its people are friendly and genuine. Tourists are made to feel like family. (Many elderly people, after visiting, decide to retire here.) Arkansans appreciate their lovely, natural state. They protect the environment. Arkansas air and water are clean and pure.

Football fans across the state root for the Arkansas Razorbacks.

There aren't any major league sports teams in Arkansas; most people travel to nearby Texas or Louisiana for that. However, they do get enthusiastic about high school and college sports, especially the Razorbacks, the football team of the University of Arkansas. In 1909, Coach Hugo Bezdek referred to his rowdy team as "a wild band of razorback hogs." The nickname stuck. This home team has won many championships.

An elderly country singer "jams" in Mountain View, a town in the Ozark Mountains.

The industrious and artistic people who make their homes in the isolated hills of the Ozarks rate a special mention. They have been misunderstood for years because they live in isolation. Without much money or modern conveniences, they are skilled in the art of "making do." They rely on their natural surroundings for food, clothing, and shelter. They rely on each other, too. The Great Depression of 1929 barely affected the people of the Ozarks. They just "made do" as they always have.

Ozark folks can make beautiful things out of practically anything. A stick could be whittled into a polished flute; the dye from a spinach leaf could provide rich color for a skirt. Ozark artisans are considered the very best in folk arts and crafts. People come from around the world to view and buy their handmade wares, including quilts, beeswax candles, fragrant soaps, mountain dolls (made of corn cobs, husks, apples, and hickory nuts), and musical instruments (such as pinewood fiddles, gourd banjos, and the haunting dulcimer, known as "the sound of Arkansas").

Ozark people believe in strong family and neighborly ties. Their culture honors grandmothers (called Grannies) as an almost magical source of guidance and wisdom. Neighbors used to all pitch in to build each other's houses, mostly log cabins. This "house raising" was followed by a celebratory dance. Kids enjoyed fun activities such as taffy pulls, log rolling, and turkey calling. Today, many Ozark folks work to keep these wonderful traditions alive.

WORKING IN ARKANSAS

Arkansas is the number one producer of broiler chickens and rice in the United States. Its most valuable food product is soybeans, grown on the long stretches of the Mississippi Alluvial Plain. Have you ever eaten tofu? If so, you've eaten a soybean product. Soy is in much demand as a health food. Arkansas is also the source of many other major products, such as cotton and wheat.

Logging (paper, furniture, lumber) and mining (oil, natural gas, bromine) also provide many jobs. The state produces roughly half of the world's bromine, which is used in fuels, dyes, and fire extinguishers. Arkansas is the number one producer of bauxite (for aluminum). Most mines are quartz crystal mines in the Mt. Ida area. Despite all this activity, mining represents only 1% of the total state product.

Several major manufacturing companies are located in Arkansas. Frozen yogurt distributor TCBY built its first store in Little Rock. Little Debbie ("America's #1 Snack Food!") has a manufacturing plant in Gentry. Vlasic pickles, owned by Pinnacle Foods Corp., are made in Fayetteville. Tyson Foods, the world's largest poultry packaging company, is in Springdale. Finally, the headquarters of Wal-Mart, the world's largest retailer, is in Bentonville.

Poultry farms are common in Arkansas.

Arkansas is the number one rice-producing state; more than half the nation's rice is grown there. One of the best ways to enjoy rice is in delicious rice pudding. Ask an adult for help on this recipe for Delta Rice Pudding.

DELTA RICE PUDDING

1/4 cup softened butter or margarine
1/2 cup sugar
2 eggs, separated (whites in one bowl, yolks in another)
1 cup cooked rice
1/2 teaspoon cornstarch (ask your grocer)
1/2 cup raisins
1/2 cup milk
1/2 cup jelly (optional)
2 tablespoons sugar

1. Moosh butter and sugar together (cooks call this creaming) until smooth.
2. In another bowl, beat egg yolks until light; stir in rice and cornstarch.
3. Add the rice mixture to the butter/sugar mixture. Stir in raisins and milk.
4. Pour into a buttered baking dish.
5. Bake at 350° for about 30 minutes, or until it is brown on top and soft underneath.
6. Beat jelly until runny and spread over hot pudding.
7. Using a clean bowl, beat egg whites. While beating, gradually add 2 tablespoons of sugar. When egg whites form soft peaks (without falling over), stop beating.
8. Pile egg white mixture on pudding.
9. Bake at 325° for 10 to 15 minutes or until delicately brown. Enjoy your sweet treat and then get busy washing all those bowls!

Many more people now work in the service industry, in jobs that provide a service to people rather than produce a product. Jobs in the service industry include banking, insurance, real estate, communications, and transportation, among other things. Arkansas' J. B. Hunt Transport is the largest trucking carrier in the United States. Many Arkansans also work for government facilities, such as Little Rock Air Force Base.

Other Arkansans work in tourism, which is part of the service industry. Businesses such as hotels, resorts, recreational areas, and museums couldn't exist without a healthy number of tourists (visitors from other areas). People are also needed to keep the 51 state parks and 4 state museums in good order.

TAKE A TOUR OF ARKANSAS

There are ample recreational opportunities throughout Arkansas. No matter where you are, there is a swimming or fishing hole nearby, a mountain or bluff to climb, a pioneer trail to hike, or wildlife to experience. In Arkansas, the great outdoors is always yours for the taking.

The Ozark Plateau

A good place to begin your visit is in the Ozarks, where you can tour the cold springs. Mammoth Spring is one of the largest natural springs in the United States. Eureka Springs is another town built around their springs. Often called America's Victorian Village, Eureka Springs also

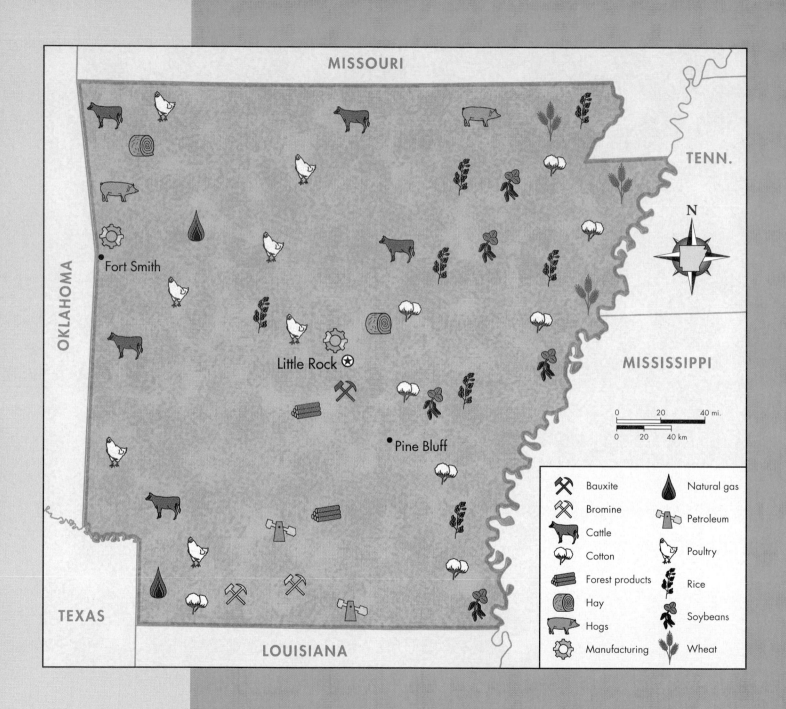

MISSOURI

TENN.

OKLAHOMA

• Fort Smith

N

Little Rock ✪

• Pine Bluff

MISSISSIPPI

0   20   40 mi.

0   20   40 km

TEXAS

LOUISIANA

Bauxite	Natural gas
Bromine	Petroleum
Cattle	Poultry
Cotton	
Forest products	Rice
Hay	Soybeans
Hogs	
Manufacturing	Wheat

62

presents the Great Passion Play, the bible story of the death of Christ. More than any other play, people in America come to this one every year, with its cast of hundreds and exotic animals.

While in the Ozarks you'll want to see if you can find some of the smokehouses, fruit houses, and corncribs the area is known for. Don't miss canoeing or white-water rafting on the Buffalo National River, one of the most beautiful natural sights in the world. Ride a horse, or go trout fishing in the White River, Spring River, or any number of smaller lakes and rivers. Gaze up at the 225-foot (69-m) waterfall at Hemmed-In Hollow.

People come from around the world to tour the Civil War sites scattered throughout the Ozarks. There's a site dedicated to the Battle of Fayetteville, as well as Prairie Grove Battlefield State Park near Fayetteville. Near Rogers is the Pea Ridge National Military Park, where one of the most important battles in the Civil War took place. To top off your historic tour, check out a working water mill at the War Eagle Mill in Springdale.

Tourists enjoy strolling through Eureka Springs Gardens, 33 acres (13 ha) of flowers, plants, and trees.

You can take a world-famous mineral bath on Boathouse Row in Hot Springs.

The Ouachita Province

The top tourist spot in the Ouachitas is Hot Springs National Park, home of the famous thermal springs. Hot Springs itself is a city with many attractions. For information about local history, stop in at the Fordyce Bathhouse Visitor Center, which has a thermal bathing museum, or the Arkansas Walk of Fame, complete with plaques honoring famous Arkansans such as former United States president Bill Clinton. Bill Clinton sites are marked throughout Hot Springs—everything from his boyhood homes to his high school to his favorite hamburger hangout.

More Hot Springs attractions include: The Mid-America Science Museum, Magic Springs theme park (complete with the Arkansas Twister roller coaster if you dare), and Crystal Falls water park. If you can't decide what to visit first, why not climb the Hot Springs Mountain Tower? This 216-foot (66-m) observation tower offers a view of not only Hot Springs National Park but the Ouachita National Forest as well.

The West Gulf Coastal Plain

The biggest event in this area's history was the discovery of "Black Gold" in El Dorado. Black Gold is not really gold at all—it is oil. The Arkansas Museum of Natural Resources in Smackover tells the state's oil story.

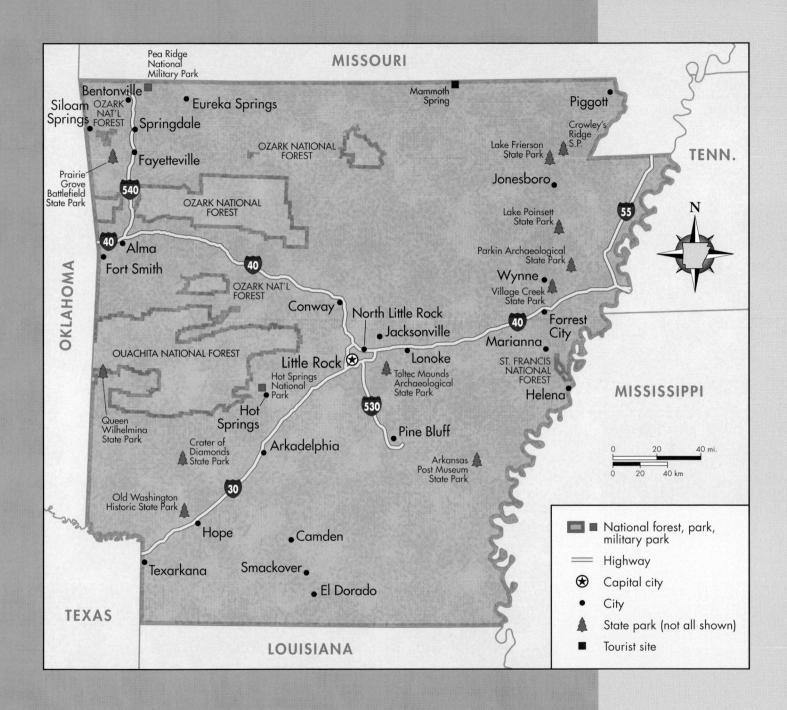

MISSOURI

Pea Ridge National Military Park

Bentonville ■

Siloam Springs

OZARK NAT'L FOREST

Eureka Springs

Springdale

Fayetteville

Prairie Grove Battlefield State Park

OZARK NATIONAL FOREST

Mammoth Spring ■

Piggott

Crowley's Ridge S.P.

Lake Frierson State Park

Jonesboro

TENN.

N

OZARK NATIONAL FOREST

540

40

Alma

Fort Smith

OKLAHOMA

OZARK NAT'L FOREST

40

Conway

Lake Poinsett State Park

Parkin Archaeological State Park

Wynne

Village Creek State Park

40

Marianna

Forrest City

55

OUACHITA NATIONAL FOREST

North Little Rock

Jacksonville

Little Rock ✪

Hot Springs National Park

Hot Springs

Lonoke

Toltec Mounds Archaeological State Park

530

ST. FRANCIS NATIONAL FOREST

Helena

MISSISSIPPI

Queen Wilhelmina State Park

Crater of Diamonds State Park

Arkadelphia

Pine Bluff

Arkansas Post Museum State Park

30

Old Washington Historic State Park

Hope

Camden

Smackover

Texarkana

El Dorado

TEXAS

LOUISIANA

0   20   40 mi.
0   20   40 km

National forest, park, military park

Highway

✪ Capital city

• City

State park (not all shown)

■ Tourist site

Murals decorate the walls of many buildings in Pine Bluff.

WHO'S WHO IN ARKANSAS?

Johnny Cash (1932–) is a Grammy award-winning country singer known around the world. He has sold more than 50 million records and recorded more than 1,500 songs. Cash was born in Kingsland.

Pine Bluff is the biggest city in the West Gulf Coastal Plain. It is called the City of Murals because more than a dozen murals (large paintings on the sides of buildings) decorate the downtown area. Pine Bluff is home to the Arkansas Entertainers Hall of Fame, a museum dedicated to honoring Arkansas' distinguished performing artists. You can see guitars, photographs, clothing, and other articles that belonged to stars such as Johnny Cash, Mary Steenburgen, and Conway Twitty. The Arkansas Railroad Museum, also in Pine Bluff, has Engine 819 on display. This famous steam engine was "queen of the rails" on the St. Louis-Southwestern Railway during the 1800s.

Old Washington Historic State Park is the site of the former Confederate capital during the Civil War. This park contains a preserved 19th-century town. More Civil War sites are the Civil War Battleground State

Parks in Poison Spring, the preserved site of the Red River Campaign, and the McCollum-Chidester House in Camden, home of Colonel Chidester, who was accused of being a Confederate spy during the Civil War.

In the twin cities of Texarkana, you can learn about the Wild West period by visiting the Ace of Clubs House, a gambling establishment built in 1885. Be sure to visit the Texarkana Historical Museum to see the Caddo Native American artifacts. Texarkana also honored its hometown musical hero, Scott Joplin, with a mural.

The Mississippi Alluvial Plain

All of Arkansas offers recreational opportunities, but Crowley's Ridge is the favorite of many. Crowley's Ridge State Park, north of Jonesboro, is a great place for camping, hiking, and picnicking. Crowley's Ridge Parkway contains Lake Frierson State Park, which has a 350-acre (142-ha) fishing lake.

East of the parkway is Parkin Archeological State Park, the very site where Hernando de Soto became the first European in Arkansas. Parkin Archeological State Park offers a visitor's center with exhibits on the Parkin Native Americans, as well as guided tours and archaeological excavations (digs). Who knows what you might find!

A family examines artifacts of the Parkin people, who were residents of early Arkansas.

In the city of Jonesboro you will find Arkansas State University. The school was founded in 1909 and today has more than 15,000 students. The university also has campuses in Mountain Home, Newport, Beebe, Heber Springs, and Marked Tree. A museum on campus has exhibits about the cultural and natural history of Arkansas.

Marianna, one of the oldest towns in Arkansas, leads to the St. Francis National Forest. The river town of Helena features many lovely old homes in both the antebellum (before the Civil War) and Victorian (after the Civil War) styles. Helena also contains the Delta Cultural Center, which tells the story of the Mississippi Delta region and its culture, including blues and gospel music. If you like to sing the blues, the King Biscuit Blues Festival is held in Helena every October.

There's more history at the Arkansas Post National Memorial south of Gillett. This memorial preserves the 1819 site of the first European settlement. Two miles away, the Arkansas Post Museum State Park features exhibits on life during frontier times. Finally, visit Toltec Mounds Archeological State Park near Scott, where you can see Native American mounds that were built centuries ago.

Exhibits about Arkansas history can be found at Arkansas Post Museum State Park.

Wherever you may be in Arkansas, you are near adventure. Be on the watch for historic Civil War sites and remnants of ancient Native American villages. Dig for diamonds. Strike oil. Be your own guide, like Arkansans of the past. Arkansas awaits you!

ARKANSAS ALMANAC

Statehood date and number: June 15, 1836/25th

State seal: The state seal is a green circle. In the middle is a bald eagle with a banner reading "Regnat Populus" (The People Rule) in its beak. Below the eagle is a shield with symbols of Arkansas' industrial and agricultural wealth. To its left is the Angel of Mercy. To its right is the sword of justice. Above is the Goddess of Liberty. Adopted in 1836; revised in 1864 and 1907.

State flag: The state flag is red with a blue and white quadrangle (four-sided figure) in the middle. Small white stars border the quadrangle; one large blue star appears above the name of Arkansas and three appear below. Adopted in 1913.

Geographic center: Pulaski, 12 miles northwest of Little Rock

Total area/rank: 53,187 square miles (137,754 sq km)/28th

Borders: Tennessee, Mississippi, Louisiana, Texas, Oklahoma, and Missouri

Latitude and longitude: Arkansas is located approximately between 33° and 36° 30' N and 89° 04' and 94° 42' W

Highest/lowest elevation: 2,753 feet (839 m) on Mount Magazine/55 feet (17 m) at Ouachita River

Hottest/coldest temperature: 120°F (49°C) at Ozark Station on August 10, 1936/–29°F (–34°C) at Pond Station on February 13, 1905

Land area/rank: 52,075 square miles (134,874 sq km)/27th

Inland water area/rank: 1,107 square miles (2,867 sq km)/31st

Population (2000 census)/rank: 2,673,400/33rd

Population of major cities:

    Little Rock: 183,133

    Fort Smith: 80,268

    Pine Bluff: 55,085

Origin of state name: From the Algonquian name for the Quapaw people, *Akansea*, meaning "southwind."

State capital: Little Rock

Previous capitals: Arkansas Post, Old Washington (the confederacy capital)

Counties: 75

State government: 35 senators, 100 representatives

Major rivers/lakes: Arkansas River, Mississippi River, Buffalo National River, Lake Chicot

Farm products: Rice, soybeans, corn, cotton, wheat, poultry, catfish, tomatoes, and milk

Manufactured products: Paper, steel, plastics, furniture, chemicals, boats, motors, and tools

Mining products: Gems, oil, petroleum, natural gas, bromine, and bauxite

Fishing products: Trout, bass, bream, crappie, walleye, and sturgeon

Anthem: "Arkansas" by Eva Ware Barnett

Bird: Mockingbird

Beverage: Milk

Dance: Square dance

Flower: Apple Blossom

Instrument: Fiddle

Motto: Regnat Populus (The People Rule)

Nicknames: the Natural State, Razorbacks, Land of Opportunity, the Bear State, the Wonder State

Song: "Arkansas," written by Wayland Holyfield; and "Oh, Arkansas," by Terry Rose and Gary Klaff

State historic song: "The Arkansas Traveler," written by Colonel Sanford (Sandy) Faulkner

Tree: Pine

Wildlife: Bald eagles, woodpeckers, snakes, bears, turkeys, geese, quail, bobcats, coyotes, armadillos, deer, and elk

TIMELINE

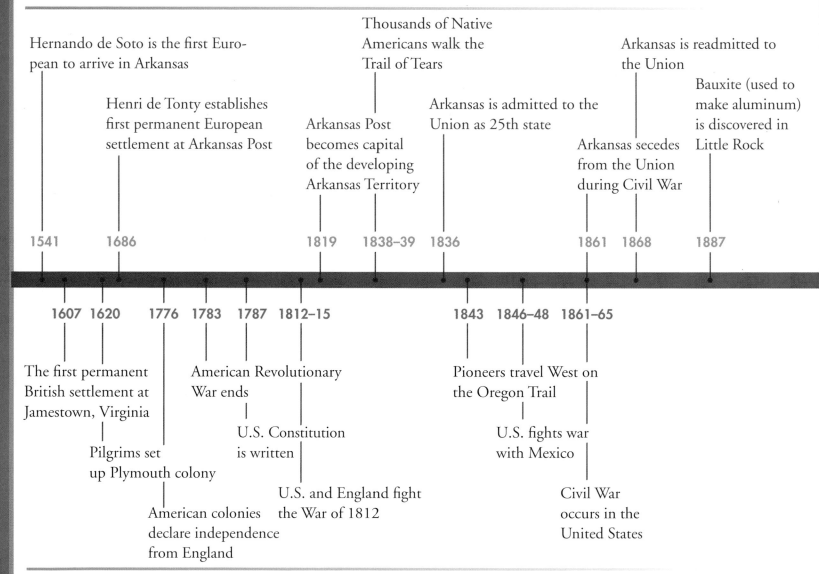

ARKANSAS STATE HISTORY

Hernando de Soto is the first European to arrive in Arkansas

Henri de Tonty establishes first permanent European settlement at Arkansas Post

Arkansas Post becomes capital of the developing Arkansas Territory

Thousands of Native Americans walk the Trail of Tears

Arkansas is admitted to the Union as 25th state

Arkansas is readmitted to the Union

Arkansas secedes from the Union during Civil War

Bauxite (used to make aluminum) is discovered in Little Rock

1541   1686   1819   1838–39   1836   1861   1868   1887

1607 1620   1776 1783 1787 1812–15   1843 1846–48 1861–65

The first permanent British settlement at Jamestown, Virginia

American Revolutionary War ends

Pioneers travel West on the Oregon Trail

Pilgrims set up Plymouth colony

U.S. Constitution is written

U.S. fights war with Mexico

American colonies declare independence from England

U.S. and England fight the War of 1812

Civil War occurs in the United States

UNITED STATES HISTORY

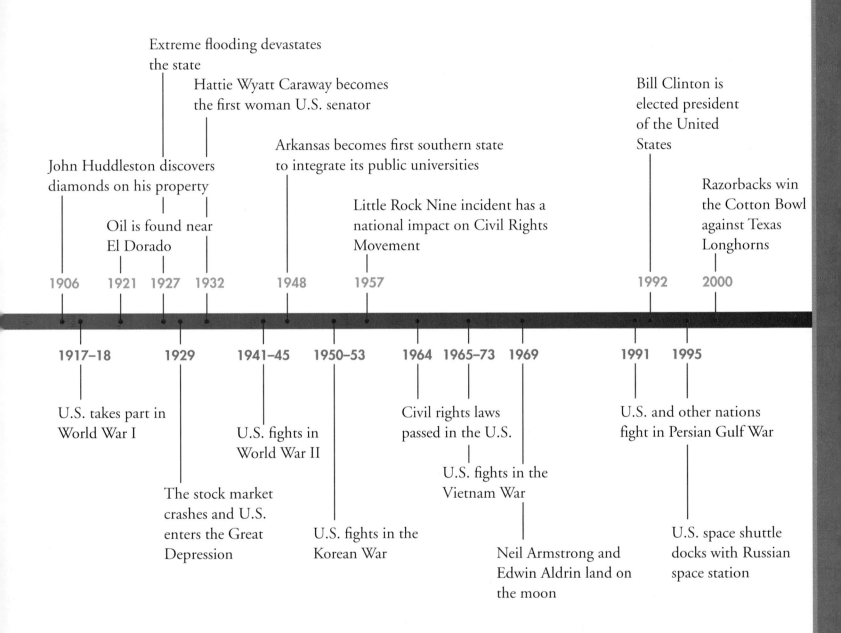

Extreme flooding devastates
the state

Hattie Wyatt Caraway becomes
the first woman U.S. senator

Bill Clinton is
elected president
of the United
States

John Huddleston discovers
diamonds on his property

Arkansas becomes first southern state
to integrate its public universities

Razorbacks win
the Cotton Bowl
against Texas
Longhorns

Oil is found near
El Dorado

Little Rock Nine incident has a
national impact on Civil Rights
Movement

1906   1921   1927   1932   1948   1957   1992   2000

1917–18   1929   1941–45   1950–53   1964 1965–73 1969   1991   1995

U.S. takes part in
World War I

U.S. fights in
World War II

Civil rights laws
passed in the U.S.

U.S. and other nations
fight in Persian Gulf War

U.S. fights in the
Vietnam War

The stock market
crashes and U.S.
enters the Great
Depression

U.S. fights in the
Korean War

Neil Armstrong and
Edwin Aldrin land on
the moon

U.S. space shuttle
docks with Russian
space station

73

GALLERY OF FAMOUS ARKANSANS

Maya Angelou
(1928–)
Bestselling author and poet. Her book, *I Know Why the Caged Bird Sings*, describes her childhood in Stamps.

Gilbert "Bronco Billy" Maxwell Anderson
(1880–1971)
Actor, director, and Oscar winner for his special contributions to the film industry. Born in Little Rock and raised in Pine Bluff.

Lou Brock
(1939–)
Baseball player for the Chicago Cubs and the St. Louis Cardinals. He held the major league baseball base-stealing record (938 total, 118 in one season). Born in El Dorado.

Eldridge Cleaver
(1935–1998)
Author and leader of the militant Black Panther Party (an organization for the empowerment of African-Americans) in the 1960s. Born in Wabbaseka.

Johnnie Bryan (J. B.) Hunt
(1927–)
Founder of J. B. Hunt Transport Services, Inc., one of North America's largest trucking companies. Born to a family of sharecroppers, Hunt later became one of the wealthiest people in America. Grew up in north central and eastern Arkansas.

E. Fay Jones
(1921–)
World-renowned architect. He designed the famous Thorncrown Chapel in Eureka Springs. Lives in Fayetteville.

Jerry Jones
(1942–)
Champion Razorback from the University of Arkansas. He went on to become a successful businessman in the oil and gas industry and the owner of the Dallas Cowboys football team. From Rose City in North Little Rock.

Scott Joplin
(1868–1917)
Well-known piano-player and composer. He specialized in a lively style of piano known as ragtime. Joplin became famous as the "King of Ragtime." From Texarkana.

Scottie Pippen
(1965–)
Chicago Bulls All-Star and one of the 50 greatest players in NBA history. He played basketball for the University of Central Arkansas. Born in Hamburg.

GLOSSARY

alluvial: rich, fertile deposits left from flooding, as in alluvial soil

antebellum: existing before the Civil War

carpetbaggers: land investors (mostly Northerners) who took advantage of Southern misfortunes during Reconstruction; known for carrying their worldly possessions in a cloth bag

discrimination: to treat someone unfavorably because of their membership in a group (usually based on race)

economy: the state of financial well-being

erosion: the gradual wearing away of land by water, wind, or ice

Fortune 500: refers to the top 500 companies in the United States

integration: combining or blending of different groups, usually cultural

malaria: disease of the blood which causes extreme chills, fever

mythical: imaginary or nonexistent

plateau: a leveled-off mountainous area

renovate: to make a structure look new again

segregation: keeping different groups, usually racial, separate from each other

terrain: the earth's surface of a geographical area

thermal: refers to hot, underground water of thermal springs

tourism: the business of providing food, shelter, and entertainment for visitors

FOR MORE INFORMATION

Web sites

State Park Junior Naturalist Program
www.arkansaskids.com
A web site full of adventures for kids in Arkansas.

The Arkansas History Commission and State Archives
www.ark-ives.com/
Includes information about the state symbols and history.

Vacation in the Natural State
www.arkansas.com
Information about tourist attractions in Arkansas, including outdoor adventures, sports, and history.

Books

Cwiklik, Robert. *Bill Clinton: President of the 90s* (Gateway Biographies). Brookfield, CT: Copper Beech Books, 1997.

Gutman, Bill. *Scottie Pippen: The Do-Everything Superstar*. Brookfield, CT: Millbrook Press, 1997.

Kelso, Richard. *Days of Courage: The Little Rock Story (Stories of America)*. New York, NY: Raintree/Steck Vaughn, 1993.

Murphy, Jim. *Boys War: Confederate and Union Soldiers Talk About the Civil War*. New York, NY: Clarion Books, 1993.

Sakurai, Gail. *The Louisiana Purchase* (Cornerstones of Freedom). Danbury, CT: Children's Press, 1998.

Stein, R. Conrad. *The Trail of Tears*. Danbury, CT: Children's Press, 1993.

Addresses

Arkansas Department of Parks and Tourism
One Capitol Mall
Little Rock, AR 72201

Governor of Arkansas
State Capitol
Little Rock, AR 72201

INDEX

ABOUT THE AUTHOR

Ellen Macaulay is a native Californian, but as soon as she began doing research on Arkansas she was hooked. She sent away for all the information she could get. Once she got to work, she discovered Arkansas' people and history were just as colorful as their landscape. Ellen would like to extend her special thanks to: Charles Durnette and Mark Christ (*milhistory@aristotle.net*) for help with war facts, her friend, Margaret Reeves, and Margaret's twin sister, Joan Wakefield, and Ann-Marie Imbornoni (*www.infoplease.com*) for gathering general research materials, and, finally a big hug for Elizabeth Danley of the Arkansas State Library for pitching in at the last second to tie up all loose ends. Ellen would also like to acknowledge her superb family for their love and support.

Photographs © 2002: AllSport USA/Getty Images/Ronald Martinez: 57; AP/Wide World Photos: 49 (Danny Johnston), 66 left (TBS), 39; Arkansas Democrat-Gazette: 25 bottom; Arkansas Department of Parks & Tourism/Chuck Haralson: 17, 67, 69; Arkansas History Commission: 36, 44; Arthur Shilstone: 27; Brown Brothers: 43; Buddy Mays/Travel Stock: 3 left, 4, 12, 13, 58, 70 right; Corbis Images: 25 top, 40, 55 (Bettmann), 56 (Annie Griffiths Belt), 74 top (Reuters NewMedia Inc.), 33, 35; Getty Images: 68 (John F. Focht), 61 (Wesley Hitt/Liaison); H. Armstrong Roberts, Inc.: 52 (H. Abernathy), 9 (G.L. French); Hulton|Archive/Getty Images: 34, 38; Icon Sports Media/John McDonough: 74 bottom; MapQuest.com, Inc.: 70 bottom left; North Wind Picture Archives: 19, 22, 23, 29, 30, 32; Photo Researchers, NY: 71 right (Dennis Flaherty), 71 bottom left (MaryAnn Frazier), 11 (Carl M. Purcell); Stock Montage, Inc.: 42; Stone/Getty Images/Joseph Sohm: 47, 50 background; Superstock, Inc.: cover, 21, 48, 59; Terry Donnelly: 7, 16, 64; The Image Works/Tom Brakefield: 15; Tom Till: 45; Unicorn Stock Photos: 53 (Dennis MacDonald), 63 (Martha McBride), 70 top left (Robert Vankirk); Viesti Collection, Inc./Robert Mitchell: 3 right, 10, 20, 66 right; Visuals Unlimited: 37 (Mark E. Gibson), 71 top left (Gary Meszaros), 8 (Henry W. Robison); www.civilwarbuff.org: 31.